ON ACCOUNT OF: SELECTED POEMS

FIELD TRANSLATION SERIES 10

Karl Krolow

ON ACCOUNT OF: SELECTED POEMS

Translated by Stuart Friebert

Introduction by Ingo Seidler

FIELD Translation Series 10

Special thanks to Karl Krolow & Suhrkamp Publishers for the right to issue these poems.

Some of the poems have appeared in the following journals: *Field, Grove, The Massachusetts Review, The Malahat Review, The Indiana Review, Antenna, The Atavist, Graham House Review, Poetry Now, Carleton Miscellany, Durak, Central Park, Yarrow, Cutbank, The Slow Loris Reader, The Barat Review, West Branch, International Poetry Review, New Letters, Quarterly West, Asylum*

The translator is also grateful to David Young and Ingo Seidler for various suggestions, and especially grateful to Karl Krolow for all his help and support.

Publication of this book was made possible through a grant from the Ohio Arts Council.

Library of Congress in Publication Data
    Krolow, Karl (translated by Stuart Friebert)
        ON ACCOUNT OF: SELECTED POEMS
        (The FIELD Translation Series; v. 10)
LC: 84-062769
ISBN: 0-932440-18-5
        0-932440-19-3

These translations are dedicated to the memory of Michael Mann, who got me started translating, and all the students it has been my pleasure to work with in more than ten years of teaching Translation Workshop at Oberlin . . .

CONTENTS

III   *The Inner Fool*

INTRODUCTION
By Ingo Seidler

I.

At the age of seventy Karl Krolow has been an active poet for nearly half a century. His more than twenty volumes of verse, each with a recognizable face of its own, reflect the development of German poetry since the Second World War as no other single literary ouevre does. Krolow has been part of, has led, has followed or opposed, all the main currents of this period, and he has done so both as a poet and as a highly regarded critic. Besides poems and critical essays he has produced reviews, some autobiographical accounts and diaries. He has also translated, to great acclaim, from the French, the Spanish and the American, and he has edited more than one anthology of poems. At the same time, he has never "committed a novel", or even a short story, and has never written a play — not even one of those lucrative radio plays that many a German poet has lived by. Although he has occasionally given lectures or seminars at the universities in Frankfurt and Munich, he has never held a permanent academic or other professional position — he is that rare phenomenon, a free lance writer who has succeeded in basing his life and his livelihood on the writing of poems and criticism. While the first half of this life was spent in the North of Germany (Hannover, where he was born in 1915, and Göttingen, where he attended the university), since 1956 he has made Darmstadt his home. Krolow has never lacked recognition or honors; he has been the recipient, at one time or other, of virtually every one of the many prizes that a German poet is eligible for, including the most prestigious of them, the Georg-Büchner-Preis (1956), and he has served as president of the German Academy for Language and Poetry (1972).

What is especially impressive about this long and illustrious career is, for one, the fact that it seems by no means finished — Krolow's productivity is as high as ever. For another, far from repeating himself or falling into a comfortable routine, in his recent volumes he has added new and surprising facets. At the same time, this development has also shown a deeper organic unity — a "Dauer im Wechsel", as Goethe would say — that allows even Krolow's most unexpected twists and turns to be interpreted as growing out of a recognizable personal potential.

Krolow started out in the wake of Oskar Loerke and, even more, Wilhelm Lehmann, poets of "Naturlyrik," both of them, and Krolow's earliest poems were certainly part of that "school" of recreating, with sensitivity and precision, bucolic scenes and complex images of the natural world. Lightness of touch and an elegant sense of proportion kept his verse from becoming overgrown with botanical details or suffocated by other visual perceptions. Not personal expression but objective recreation, a sympathetic continuing of natural processes and cycles, was the intention. The "aperspectivism" that Krolow recognized in his two models, a sovereign and unpredictable way of manipulating time and space, allowed for considerable complexity in such poems; it also made it easy for Krolow to move, under the impact of his own early translations from the French and Spanish, toward a more radical freedom of metaphorical expression. It was this act of quasi Surrealist liberation, helped along by Krolow's translations and their technical lessons, that brought about a first high point in the poet's own development, as well as exerting a very beneficial influence on the German poetic scene at large. When, in the late fifties, poetry in

11

Germany again veered towards the metaphysical — and often pretentious — it was Krolow's own poetic practice, his lightness of touch, his persistent concreteness, his intellectual grace and charm, that gently modified such trends. "German poems," he was to say, "always seem to want too much — they tend to be too heavy, or too artificial, or at any rate not discreet enough for my taste." Even the hymns, odes and elegies which he produced in those years, after a late critical encounter with Hölderlin and Trakl, still show the working of a light hand; they are airy structures, "porous" (one of Krolow's favorite adjectives) and elegant. His need for transpiration, he once explained, was never very high.

Nor was he willing to make poetry the handmaiden of politics when, during the sixties, that became the fashion. Although never afraid of taking a stand on public issues, and despite occasionally admitting references to Korea or Hungary, war and peace, might and right, into his poetry, the notion that poems might change something in "the real world" has never elicited much faith from him. Even during the period when "usefulness" and "practical relevance" became the foremost criteria applied to literary productions, Krolow was always content with Wilhelm Lehmann's "wisdom of purposelessness." No one has ever convinced him that either politics or literature were likely to gain from a forced marriage — a scepticism that would clearly not do justice to either Brecht or Enzensberger, Fried or Jandl, Kunert or even Celan. It does, however, say something about Krolow's own work; his occasional attempts at the long, wordier, public statement in verse were no more than a succès d'estime. His readership may have diminished in those years, but his status as a poet's poet did not suffer — a fact to which the many critical tributes by fellow poets testify. In the drawn out controversy about long (and "public") vs. short ("private") poems that went through German literary magazines in the sixties, Krolow predictably emerged as the eloquent advocate of the brief, the condensed and suggestive poem.

II

The present anthology offers poems from the last twenty-five years of Krolow's work. They come from some ten different volumes and they pick up where the H. Salinger (1968 and 1969) and the M. Bullock (1969) translations left off.

With two small exceptions (of which a few words later) the selection can thus claim to be a full and fair introduction, for the English reader, to the second half of Krolow's work; the crucial seventies are especially well represented.

It was then that Krolow entered into what critics have called the period of his late parlando style: brief sentences seemingly effortless and artless, a mosaic of everyday expressions, but shot through with flashing concetti and distancing ironies. Frequent ellipses make these poems shorter and shorter; reductions in contents, emotion, and empathy render them laconic, cooled off, even dry at times. As Krolow himself notes, "Slowly all feeling disappears from our sentences." True enough — but strangely in contradiction with another fact about this late phase. For one can also note a subtle increase in personal expression in these late poems — the very opposite in a sense from what one might expect. Most poets, after all, start out with an acute need for self-expression in their youth and later slowly move towards more objective methods; with Krolow, paradoxically, the very opposite seems to hold true. Personal concerns now make a consistent though unobtrusive appearance: memories, accumulated over the decades, reflections, fears and hopes, fragments and hints of philosophical musings, awareness of bodily functions and frailties ("body — a sketch designed against decay"), time and its "lazy conspiracy," old age, depressions, and death. Even such dark and personal themes are presented, it is true, in a manner curiously devoid of self-pity or sentimentality: they are the stuff from which poetry is fashioned, and the spirit of this precise operation is one of self-irony, scepticism, and amused wonderment. Discretion is still an important virtue; even now there is great reluctance to use the word "I". In its place the impersonal German "man" (one, we, you, they, according to context) is the form most often employed also in these late poems. But it is increasingly clear that the poet himself and his perspective is now in or behind these seemingly neutral lines, more so, at any rate, than in Krolow's earlier work. Everyday objects and events provide the starting point for many of these late sketches, written, one is given to understand, on half sheets of paper and almost never worked on later: these are records of the "poetic act" (Valéry) as much as poems in a more traditional sense. In Krolow's own words, he starts from "What anybody can see or hear all around . . .

15

habits like washing one's hands or crossing the street, not worth mentioning in a way, but not worth leaving out either, worth noting, jotting down: such common things are used as quarries for poems." There is still a kind of hypertrophy of the visual ("quiet in all but the eyes"), even though, compared to the flamboyant earlier work, the vision has sobered considerably: "The magic lamp behind your eyes has died away." After the delicate reconstructions of nature in his early work and the dazzling metaphors of his middle period, Krolow has entered a third phase, both more personal and more sober than one might have expected. Simplification, perhaps even impoverishment, on the technical level is proportionally matched by an enrichment of existential perspective. Krolow's recent excursions into the field of autobiographical prose seem to be another expression of the same change of attitude, an increased interest in the poetic self, that has brought Krolow's development full circle: from the reverently objective via the flamboyantly creative to the ironically subjective.

There are only two aspects of Krolow's later development which the present volume does not document, a formal one and a thematic one, both slightly extravagant detours. The first of these is the poet's short-lived experiment of returning to venerable, but long abandoned and disused, strict forms: sonnet and terza rima, rondels and rondeaux, sicilianas and sestinas, and above all, rhymes again, rhymes everywhere, after twenty years of virtual abstinency. Krolow's own comment ("As if one could forget the entire twentieth century") is only half true, for the language that fills these old, academic forms is provocatively contemporary, even slangy, not just twentieth century, but quite clearly of the eighties. The fact that Krolow has discontinued this mode in the volumes following *Herbstsonett mit Hegel* (1981) suggests that he, too, was not convinced by the results: the wheel of history cannot be turned back — not even, it seems, *half* the wheel . . . The other detour in Krolow's late work that did not find its way into the present collection concerns a volume, published in 1970 under the pseudonym of Karol Kröpcke and entitled *Bürgerliche Gedichte* (Middle Class Poems). The treatment of sex (much the central topic in the volume) aroused considerable indignation — not only because of the high degree of explicitness, but also because of its combining sex with extreme forms of violence. The title is, of course, doubly or triply ironic: does it claim to offer what the middle class *wants* to read? Or what they will wax pleasurably *indignant* about? What describes their *phantasies*? Or what they object to, vainly and guiltily, as they continue watching its commercial equivalent on television? What the shocked bourgeois critics failed to acknowledge was the fact that Krolow was only joining a most illustrious club of poets, *German* poets at that, who had all on occasion written pornographic verse, a club that counts among its members Lessing and Wieland, Goethe and Schiller, Bürger and Voss, Stolberg and Schlegel, Heine and Brecht. No doubt, Krolow's crudely erotic "bourgeois poems" are strong tobacco, but no doubt again, they are well made examples of a fairly neglected genre, highly successful exercises in calling a spade a spade.

An outstanding translator of ambitious verse himself, Krolow has nevertheless concluded that *resignation* is the translator's proper muse. If the poet's own achievements refute such scepticism, so does the present volume. Its lively and precise renderings, idiomatic but poetic, scrupulous yet graceful, smack neither of resignation nor of wilfulness or — traduttore/traditore —

of treason. What they do suggest is the cheerful
— and highly competent — playing of the second fiddle by one who is well versed in playing
the first. And those are, of course, the only fiddlers that will transpose a tune without doing
harm to it.

I   WE LIVED PRETTY WELL

PSYCHIC STORIES

Nothing's wrong. No one's
outwitted. One likes to eat
and sleep, keep
to the average.
What's wrong? What's eluded us?
Of course there are also
psychic stories.
And that's the hard part.
Suddenly there's no
deceiving yourself.
Feeling's involved, among other things.
Your blood pressure changes
really quickly.
And in no time, fear
turns up, it's lost its tongue.
You don't know if
you should make a move.
You don't move.
The terror doesn't make a sound.

I'M NOT TOO GOOD

I'm not too good
for some things that could happen.
Nothing's happening, no
silent movie with a plot
that's too thick, disappearing
politely behind an unknown director.
Of course there's no blood
on my desk —
I'm not writing down
what I lost in a dependent clause
or at the third ring
of my apartment door.
Nothing's happening, I don't want
to save the world. I'm just trying
to get through enemy lines
with my words.
So sometimes my fingers
grow through strange hair
and every day
I'll get myself some death
any way I can.

KEEPING ON GOING

I go around some street corners
and have an idea in my head clear as a picture
of time between March and October.
I like the cut-out
I'm moving around in,
slowly, toward change,
dying of something, while I
just keep on going, at least for the moment —
how do you write about
still being alive
among objects that are all used up
and possessions that shine,
lists without specifics, so to speak?
Some things just wait for me
to stop defending myself.
In the air
shining insects.

WHEN THINGS TURN GREEN

Anyone can call into the woods
or let old love letters spoil in the rain
at just the right moment,
dump the second car somewhere, forever —
and take a false name
like an abandoned child.
You'd like to put that down
to spring.
But it happens too fast.
The revolution's begun,
the leaves breathe too hurriedly,
nobody protests the development
of the subconscious,
street numbers disappear overnight.
It's hard to find anyone
who knows his way around in the green.

TALKING-WRITING

Who's talking? Writing? Let it
come to that, just keep wearing
your natural hair, when
you ask me what I think.
I'm left-handed. It's
different with me.
I turn off, when you ask me;
I'm up ahead, out of the picture.
Things get serious if there's
a false move, when you show
people your list of requests.
That's like turning on
the light suddenly.
Everyone wants to see something.
It's like the beginning of spring.
You can't get rid of the smell
of violets on your clothes.

LANDSCAPE FOR MYSELF

I

Look
for minerals and adjectives
in it.

Shadows of trees
allow you to describe them
several ways.

Noon devours
a fish with a geometrical fin
in the shadows.

My landscape makes me
hungry as wind.

People with long arms
reach the sky.

Tired birds
sleep on the air.

Hands
holding colored fruit
out of habit.

The tradition of long twilights.

Night glows;
a heap of charcoal.

II

The believable beauty
of a column of smoke.

Conscience
has the voice of an echo
on the horizon.

Quartertones of a melody
from willowwood:

excited noise
loses itself, like mothflight.

The surface of black olives,
arranged by Euclid, yesterday.

I let them
hang in the dry light
before my eyes.

III

Out over a salt beach
the reflection of rowboats.

Wet roses smell:
an announcement of death.

Cruises through green:
its silence
can't be transferred.

Pollen on my eyelids.

The fragile face of days
when leaves fall.
Carefully you bend down
over them.

The suicide roses smell
of past poems.

DAY AND NIGHT

The pleasure of day
and night
the chin pressed
on the breast or raised
and alive
on the whole body.
Acquaintances go by
with an inner security.
The outside world grows
easy
hours true as gold
collecting lists of things
one would like, full
of beautiful subterfuge.
No one sees through
their game, except
the light that changes
(as we all know) except
the strange future
that falls into the house.

TOGETHER

This feeling we share:
we say We.
A museum in the
first person plural,
together
and moving from hand to hand,
picking tulips and kisses,
our one breath
breathless. That happened
to us. We
were under our laprobe,
nighttravel through Germany
with the plural of Love,
of beds.
One last time we take a look
at life before it leaves us.

THE SKIN YOU'RE STUCK IN

The mechanical toy of my childhood,
Fantasy: grown quite old by now,
previously a means of not being seen.
My lamp and closet say
I live without having myself.
One gets used to the skin
one's stuck in.
Reality — a succession of images
controlled by choice.
Between times, sleep, lying beside one another,
death coming closer and closer.
She wore some sort of dress
you could see her legs and thighs through.
Forget everything. Some sort of destruction
comes closer and closer.
What'll we do with this life?

THIS AND THAT

For this and that
we leave less and less time.
Each object holds on to its place —
dishes, furniture, beds for
orgasms that are perfectly quiet.
Moving through the town that's worth seeing,
through marriage, through the grass,
through your own German.
We look at each other hurriedly
and put up with some things —
more than one day — torn
from the calendar — the same suit
with a lost body,
not breathing books in anymore,
the dust between fingers
and quiet except the eyes.

VIEW / PROSPECT

A view of little, unless
one took seriously
what sticks to clothes,
the way dust writes in furnished rooms,
and the way a child's kite has been aging
respectably in a treetop
since last fall.
A person disappears behind
a shack.
You gesture No. You know that scene,
how something stuck in its tracks
repeats itself,
like this view of nothing at all.

I'M TIRED OF

I'm tired of
the succession of things.
Simultaneity
baffles me
like pure luck
or sitting at a
long table without end,
which loses itself in the landscape,
where illusion begins.
I'm tired of
being surrounded by life.
Gaping at me.
Tearing the clothes off my body.
I'm tired of
this sort of nakedness,
the hard work and bodily mistakes,
the decay, the smell
of rotting gall-nuts.
I want to be alone
with the prick of my vein.
I'm tired of

feeling the drip of my soul
on my back
and being asked about
its origin.
Muzzle me
before I say a word.

HOW'S IT GOING?

You take it in but not unexamined:
nice weather without any catcalls.
Yes and *No* are sometimes hard
to tell apart like
a swig of virtue which
is always beneficial.
Your left hand's very quiet.
It knows what the right's leaving undone.
People with mixed emotions
are men and women
who lack something.
That's not funny.
People who can't hold to anything
get distracted, ask
"How's it going, friend?"

WE WERE YOUNG

We were young and the summer
outside town like hay high as a house.
Nights we heard people breathing
through the wall.
Each day was the beginning of a story.
We sailed along
on the soles of old shoes.
I knew nothing of
'melancholy factors'
and that proofs make sentences behave.
There was no date on a street scene.
There really was wind when
the trees rustled.
Someone fed me
a piece of cold chicken
while I couldn't get out of watching
some love-making.
Later the friendliness was huge.
In the hall a grown woman
put her huge breast in my hand.
I shoved my tongue in her mouth.
I'd grown older.

THE EFFECT OF CHEMISTRY

The effect of chemistry — a moment of sadness
appears. It's raining outside.
You have to watch the coated pills
in this dampness.
Each body is sad in its own way.
Desire grows for someone
who's not there.
It's as if a certain bird began
to sing.
No, you're not happy
going through daydreams
with people who speak a different language.
It rains in our eyes.
Misunderstandings grow
though the door is open.
Just where is it we're supposed to spend some
      time?
Dreamy democrats
stare after us.
They think
we have to love each other.

SELF-SERVICE

I serve you something to drink,
self-service, with the tenderest possible words
I dig an entrance for you into things past:
childhood scenes — remember —
a little girl letting her horse lick
her braids and the distant whistles of trains
getting lost in the trimmed bushes, so much tit-
    tering.
Ordinary life was soon smelling of canalization.
The metabolism of the seasons hung on under
    our armpits.
People struck a light note: "wonder why no one
    loves me?"
Later, their muscles grew and they held their
    heads
in a pail of water.
The windows were wet and steamy.
But the back of our head was very clear.
There was more light than we wanted,
but a sheet of wrapping paper crumbled
to yellow dust in our fingers, like reality
which used to matter —

our furniture was gaining vogue.
Suddenly nothing was there,
a mutation, voices like spots on blotting paper,
and someone told you, as if from memory,
that everything was for nothing.

INVENTED LANDSCAPE

I like having: a surveyor's map
on my knees.
Everything else's my invention:
day with its rosy dawn applied,
good weather which tastes of
bonbon,
the season, private as
leaves in the wind dancing
around our feet.
Give yourself time, I think,
fold the map.
Fantasy takes off
when maps disappear.
Rivers foam up again
with chemistry,
and a landscape's
not a movie about love.
I never ask myself
if shadows are lonely.
Rustling in the dark
I meet up with myself.
Other things look good in the light.
I feel mortal,

and sometimes singsong's
enough for happiness
when green
puts in an appearance
on a screen.

LET THE LAUGH

Let the laugh catch in your throat.
Will it rain or be nice?
Leave cheerfulness
alone, it's catching. You won't affect
the fuse ticking away in the bushes.
Sad at nothing except being in the world.
Between acts the stage is empty.
The group-therapy session was interrupted.
Nothing will enter history —
your desire for happiness, the pleasure
of lighting one cigarette with the next
or just doing nothing
in your room that smells of leaves
and feeling the way the middle class felt
in the nineteenth century.

SOME TIME AGO

Mornings it really smelled
of fresh bread in some streets.
Really. There was no progress,
no regress. Only the ivy kept
moving up the tree trunks, patiently.
The possibility of abstractions
wasn't taken seriously at all.
You could touch everything. What a glorious
    time
of high bicycles! My grammar wasn't exactly
    correct,
the way it is today. Looking out windows was
the favorite occupation.
With no supply of experience
we lived pretty well,
while in the evening I could still
make out the colors I knew.
The backside of our houses
grew black fast and I didn't realize
every day could be dangerous
and work a remedy for exhaustion.

II OUR SHORTCOMINGS

NOON

As usual there's nothing doing around here.
The clock says it's noon
just to be polite.
A delicate sound — as if life were being ex-
    ·pected,
comes up and disappears.
You're simply there.
The light's on in the sky.
The air's too sweet as usual
when the wind blows this way.
If you walk straight ahead
you'll smell pancakes.
But that could just be
the chemistry again. Workers
are taking a break now.
Your car windows are closed
and you're taking your own body
for a ride, your soul,
your happiness with a time
that's gone like landscape
come down to zero.

THE EVENING

Evening's no longer cleaning
its light with a scissors,
which is waiting for nails
to cut.
The darkness
is a shift
between the lines.
People, their mouths moist,
talk about the night they've seen.
Clothes grow heavier
before they drop.
In the white of the eye
you can recognize the poetic vein now.
Obscurantists, exhausted,
sleep standing up.

THE LOVE OF LIFE

There's gold among the trees.
Thanks to barbituates, everything's in good
    shape,
I think: this light
can't be touched.
I've still not moved
from this spot, I listen —
a delicate noise like a zipper
being opened on a blouse.
The love of life can't be described at all,
something gets messed up, and even
the first sentence isn't right.
And what else? Something or other
will darken the air.
A personal reference
enters the text. The connection
evaporates before your eyes.
An automatic nodding — all that's left.

I SEND THE ANGEL AWAY

I send the angel away,
with its feminine or masculine first name,
and instead of lighting up a cigarette
(which burns the mucus membrane in my
     mouth),
I ask myself whether there's
anything unique left: a bag
full of dope, left
standing as an oversight,
or by mistake removing your
ill-fitting body, airing it,
and thus being misunderstood.
An unembarrassed cat
climbs into the empty bed
and rolls around. Lust's
in the way you look at it
and a ticklish matter
even in the New Testament.
We're in our decline and fall,
the angels sent off,
first names changed
and the body
going silent.

THE THINGS THAT HAPPEN OUTSIDE

The things that happen outside:
trivial myths, the heat unbearable,
the cold a white line.
You draw the drapes
as long as you need to.
Why are so many afraid?
Your body suddenly grows heavy,
but then you forget it again,
smile through cigarette smoke.
We see nothing whole.
That's all just stories
like a toy you
put together out of something.
It's quiet outside,
you can just make out
the sounds of night-insects.

GROWING OLDER

1

Scratching away
the years
with your fingernail.

A lighter sleep.
The dream of short sentences.

The black Chambertin
with its memory of wine shops
which warmed your fantasy —
(its mirror sinking
in the bottle).

Living in a room
with dying letters.

A strange mouth
which robs my speech.

Patiently listening to
it calling my own name.

2

Physical changes
as painted feelings.

A tired voice
borne past
on the air —
brittle visibility.

The changing views
of what was.

There are examples
for death lived with confidence.

The wordtrap's still set.

Carefully
I move
near it.

3

Dusty travel photos —
yesterday we drove through them
without a breath.

Thin line
of sweaty love.

People carry proverbs
into my house
that live quietly
under my protection.

A few thoughts
in a bath of light
while looking at a travel brochure.

Night, that blown out candle
at my forehead.

4

Forgotten fire-line.

Some words I'll follow
a long time.

Gathering their snow
in my mouth.

The winter in the words
grows —
algebraic surface of a life
with unreachable, white
ciphers.

An equation for
what comes later.

Lonely signature.

It's still cold
under the tongue.

5

The magic lamp
behind your eyes.
went out.

Experience, enough
for this and that.

The roaring
of subterranean water —
weaker in your ear now.

Earth-time
which you can read
on an old pocket watch.

Your wandering soul
right there
on the flat of your hand.

WHO'S WHO?

We're born
without knowing how
one word follows another.
We name the weekdays
and try to get along with them.
Some skin burned, some concrete crackles.
Who's who? Simple music
comes out of old records.
We're amazed: that really existed.
In my room hung with maps
I hear other languages from long ago
as hallucination.
Sometimes we're afraid
of everything.
You laugh. You show too much
of your gums.
Sometimes our identity
grows robust.
Then we take another look
at a spot that's empty.
A little while ago
strangers slept there together.
We scarcely noticed.

Someone next to me says:
The biological processes of the organism
is all I'm interested in now.
I let him talk.

MUSIC

What I exchange for music
is an uncertain feeling.
What would you do?
Just listen and amuse yourself,
lie around or think about Soul?
There's so much we can't turn up,
it went through a sieve, disappeared
in the earth or the air.
What does that have to do with Erik Satie or
Messiaen's lascivious organs?
I can't get rid of this feeling.
It spoils the nice weather we're having out-
       doors —
a slowly falling rain.
Is it always like this, you listen
too long and can't get rid of the rain
that drenches our rational life.
My eyes fill with water
that takes my sight away.

AFTERWARD

Afterward — what is it?
Some things repeat themselves.
Lovers come together
in water, nature's too vegetal.
Something for sleepy people.
Everything's been covered by habits
that delay reactions.
Would you like a drink? Not really.
You rub the stubble on your chin,
notice nothing that's alive: not even a window
flying open.
Not one slaughtered animal cries out.
Afterward — how odd our expectations:
we can't get back
to what was, anymore.
Everything's sexless and silent.
You don't know your way around
people anymore.

SUFFICIENTLY

Everything's been sufficiently described —
how things start and go on,
what's left is just
a used-up landscape,
complicity, feelings,
good advice that's too expensive
for those who act on it.
Everything's well enough known.
No healthy picture
emerges that you can cut
out of paper
and tack on the wall.
We see our shortcomings
as charming eccentricities.
There's imaginary gold
in the streets.
Love's so near
you can grasp it,
this place has no background.
Carefully we climb
through the countryside
measured and marked by those
who acquire things
just in time.

RESTLESSNESS

Traveling with both hands: —

Moving inside
the moments, shining,
a Bengali fire.

Without weather and Sunday
our distress: —
Sound of a peacock
spreading its tail
or the small steps
between right and left.

No one seeing
to the frenzy of the shadows
that live off the light.

On the bank
between the stranded words
water talking to water.

THE END OF SOMETHING

Put a book of fairy tales
on your knees.

What was there
besides a ride through water?
The journey from
grave to grave is short.

The past's
a landscape
with women who're
quickly moving off.

The end comes
paging through pictures
no one wants
to see anymore.

MY LIFE

Chairs are arranged differently
at the end of a conversation.
I am not one of a kind.
I'm many, while hearing, suddenly,
a clock tick or
I smoke a cigarette in bed.
I didn't know that at the start.
It's like an old trick.
The bags under the eyes
show more clearly now.
As for "my life," well, there wasn't
much to it, about as little as love
can be considered an aspect of possession.
Biographical style is deceiving.
Some have
their career behind them.
I look at the little things
in the store window without buying any.
The grass we've lain in
has no secrets.
The suffering we do at moments
can't be seen.
Each day's as dangerous as

the quick flow of blood.
We live, nothing happens to us, expecting
a noise in the hallway
whose meaning we see
too late.

NO TIME TO LOSE

You have no time to lose.
The unfamiliar woman across from you
thinks: he's old.
We grew up. We changed,
we've been sleeping badly for a long time
or in an automatic way.
The world doesn't get any clearer,
while you work a music box.
A crash course in Marxism,
the meal you bolt, love
in a second-class train berth, quick,
won't change the condition
of the veins on your temple.
Sometimes waiting is good.
Perhaps a door will open
and everything's different.

I BREATHE

Some wear false eyelashes.
The seasoned world's like that.
Lots of things go wrong, so
dust sticks to clothes,
a light spot's all that's left
of dried blood,
of loving, in this fast life.
I appeal to no one,
I just breathe.
It's crazy, how wild country flowers smell.
I remember that lovely fling,
the intoxication of being very far away
from anyone I know and suddenly
in a stranger's arms.

TIME PASSING

I

Names scribbled on a blackboard
with chalk —
messages from time passing.
Eyes grow old and see
the quiet oxidization of fall.
You grope into the fog
with gouty fingers.
Things left behind
spoil in the rain: paper, clothes.
The surfaces
of your food turn moldy.
You're patient, keep watching,
your breath comes slower in the dark
in which the hours that wooed
their properties in the daylight
no longer know their way around.

II

You speak a foreign language in your sleep
while death listens.
Insect noise against the panes.
We live a while on figures of speech
and look at ourselves
in our different clothes.
It's a clever trick — waking up
every day, falling asleep again.
The motley heap of our things
lying all around.
We move past, understand nothing,
open doors, go through a room
full of women.
In different voices
we answer the same questions
over and over again.

III

We walk among the furniture.
I move inside a space
that gets tighter and tighter around me.
In this heat your mental range
becomes a wavy line a snake makes,
a ghostly apparition like
the past.
I point my finger
at what I still have
while a car driving by
wraps a dusty flag around me.
Slowly all feeling disappears
from our sentences.
The wall of the room peels away
like skin.
I leave the objects
their names.

IV

The echo of the last sentence.
Love without response —
a body wrapped in air.
All this floats past:
the movement of a woman
next to a man or
the wintergreen of some trees.
We do our work silently.
The images dissolve
into explanations.
The house I live in
grows colder.
I give up trying
to describe the seasons.

V

Time, slowed down under time's lens.
I can reflect on
how durable the flesh
of the apple grown ripe in August,
of an upper thigh.
I start from one word
and find the next.
Unversed in reading thoughts,
I've got my perceptions
vivid red, dense green.
I watch
how an object
becomes image.
No time left
for vocabulary and grammar.
It ends on a sundial
in the shade.

VI

Locked into my surroundings.
A clockface on the tower
is stuck at 11:44 —
eternity at a height of twenty meters.
The unconscious tries to express itself.
I see the bubble form
before each spoken sentence,
which emerges from a feeling,
locked into the
possibilities of my language.
My cat leaves dark
clumps of hair behind.
Daily I lose hair
from various places on my body.
I won't go naked
when it's my turn.

VII

Who's talking with my mouth?
I hear the expression of my perceptions.
The automatic watch on my left forearm,
waterproof, shining
during nights of wet love.
I have this body
which is a sight for some,
thereafter a memory for a
mind slowly letting up,
in the constant darkness of
whatever's disappeared.

VIII

Quick succession of images. Scattered pieces of
    clothing.
Never again sleeping together.
You were about to put it differently.
Waking up and having enough,
parting forever.
Laughter coming from trees.
Strange hair tangling with yours.
Chairs scraping, fingers entwined,
curiosity perhaps, but nothing
you'd turn around for.
I lived with my skin which sweat,
which you dried.

IX

I know that this . . .
Smell of tobacco from a jacket.
What can you depend on?
Only for a moment
the way a woman looks
whose legs I spread.
Only for a moment do I know,
can I say, what a . .
I turn my head
to a landscape drawing by.
Several clocks strike at once.
For a moment
time's discernible.
I know it's so.

X

In this hand that's mine
I feel pain.
In vain I try
to ignore someone's passion.
I give in.
The shining. The soft movements.
Simply in some hotel or other.
Maybe I'm dreaming,
an argument you can quickly refute.
Your heart can't catch the clock.
Time relentlessly shifting.
(The indisputability, on the other hand,
of a mathematical proposition.)
Lines under her eyes,
under his mouth.
The clock works quickly
through the night.

XI

Application of language —
he brought the bottle to his mouth.
You're not supposed to drink like that.
I can only describe the process
if I know
how dry his lips were.
The minute-hand
advances in earnest.
The tiny time semen takes to flow.
Flecks of albumen
on a clock-face,
edged in yellow.
Fingers trying to understand each other.
Finally you scratch it away
with your thumbnail.

XII

A picture of connections, drawn while sleep-
    walking.
The spotted pink and white of shrubs
in a garden you recognize again.
The physiological weakness of our ability to
    observe.
All sentences have the same value.
Your pulse keeps changing
while smoking and writing
and you let your body burn, it's all
that alcohol, your mucus membranes are on fire.
Your body stretches out so quietly
in the cold air of the room.
We all do that — wait.
Here, here's a light.

XIII

I'm not certain whether for some time I've . . .
There's always the sketching
on the skin of a stranger.
You have to keep your head
at the same height.
There's bathing in the sweat
of another's body, sharing
your words with
someone else for a while, looking
at intentions for a while, which
you both get rid of and talk
with your thighs
as if that were the way.

XIV

The personal poem
of our bodies —
We fall back on our dreams.
In the meantime, there's a life
not shared with anyone.
You always meet by chance.
There's so much time to settle
your account with the world —
arcades through the leaves,
doors open to heaven, there
where no one's ever been,
and nothing for your arms to hold
anymore, to pass the time.

XV

It's best to keep quiet, you know.
Death is not an imaginary person.
I talk in those hours
in which I'm not alive.
The end's weightless —
a stranger's hands
lay on the covers.
Our body, lightened, relieved,
disappears in a few hours —
a disguised opportunity
to say goodbye.
I look at my task.
When you do drop over
your head's usually ahead.

III THE INNER FOOL

NEW LIFE

Blue appears
like Mörike's soft harp notes.
Over and over
that will be so.
The people paint
their houses.
The sun shines
on the various walls.
Everyone expects it to.
Spring, yes, it's you!
You can read all about it.
The green hedge is a quote
from an unknown poet.

The people paint
their families too, their cars,
their boats,
their new life
is pleasing to all.

RAIN

Rain like
too-long sentences
in a dead language,
Cicero's Latin.

Salamander-time.
Warm bodies
starting to freeze.

Someone bending
over damp paper
trying to describe
the funeral of the light.

Snail tracks persist,
the way old people
remember the old days.

IN THE HEAT OF NOON

Heat — an animal
with a pink tongue.

One body casting its shadow
waves to another.

Slowly it moves
through the incomplete
story of noon.

Platonic idea
of coolness.

A fountain distributing
traces of moisture.
Its linguistic water
went dumb —
the lack of communication —

Fairy-tales start
with a dryness
in the throat.

I SEE THINGS DIFFERENTLY

I see things differently —
words are remains
of capitalism —
I don't see it that way.
I say *snow* and have
the winter of '29 in my mouth.
Water, I say drowning
in the North Sea again.
Fire. My hand's
been burning since
the last war.
I say *freedom* and
still don't know what I mean.

TIME

Time: something
that makes our pockets
wet with blood.

Life's raining
out of open bodies.

The days, and
the quiet business they do
with people who go
astray.

One month painting
its image in the sand
for the next,
with no relation
to what comes.

No sort of beautiful weather
can alter a cancer.

Neatly ordered papers
burn, year after year.

GRADUALLY

Gradually, the images disappear and rheumatic
    hands
lay hold of whatever they still can.
This place has been snapped to death and nothing
    shines
over the details anymore. What's the point in
    distinguishing?
I read something or other: half a page long or as
    far
as I get, arrive at zero, a slot machine
that's quiet now, or something like a craze
that's been hushed. All I still feel
is the pressure of shoes on my feet.
That's acceptable, I think, and realize: desire
comes from the brain and not
from a body that fits you badly, just happens
to stand straight as a candle or leans over a table.
There are still some of us who understand that:
life's off somewhere and we just smile like a
    wind-up doll
and think to ourselves: the others know this too.
An insect's appetite for the unknown
is poison for the metabolic system. And there's
    burning

in our eyes that try to follow
our own transparent fingers spreading into the
    air.

MAY

Physiology time.

Everyone gets
another mouth
and new fingers.

A body's a home.

Minutes spent loving
the view: young animals,
bushes and girls
in see-through clothes.

The colored zone of a face.

Esperanto of air
visited by birds.

Proverbs come true.

The memory of the coolness:
a stack of white papers.

SOME EXCEPTIONS

When someone calls for help
and people actually stop, when
someone's telephoning loudly about
you in the house next door
and you weren't warned
about it before,
when in the warm nights
the vines defy all nightingales,
when they still wear brassieres
under their blouse,
when false teeth
smile back sweetly,
when concrete melts
like Dali's watches,
when those who've come up short
show up with
long tools,
when tenderness
comes from rinse water,
when you're megalomaniacal
and keep very still,
when jealousy even casts
suspicion on female house pets,

when a falling razor blade
cuts nothing but air,
when I imagine
everything going on
with *when*, without *but*.

ANTIQUITY

It rains pigeons for photographers.
The latinate air
sleeps over the fire
of the chestnut-vendors.

You can wear stiff hats,
a storm will never come up.

Kisses and bonbons
grow in every mouth,
as in an opera by Paisiello.

Tell me, finally, you've
had enough of all that.

For a long time Night's
been standing with black thighs
at the door.

She leads you
to open graves.

Antiquity's alive in them
with blood long since congealed.

LOOK AT THAT, WILL YOU

Look at that, will you, could
be someone simply going off,
out of his worldly life,
after he'd washed his mouth
with the leftover Saint Emilion,
politely disappearing, didn't panic
looking ahead to his exit, asked
himself for the first time what he
was doing here with the others, who
were managing without even thinking.
Nobody gave him the fire to live on,
and the sensual revolution
brought no relief.
From this moment on
he didn't have a tough time
saying to himself that
it'd make damn little difference
which direction you
disappeared in.

FOREVER

Losing time, forever.
Snow starts falling
around me, forever.
No way home, no way back.
That's as simple as
letting yourself fall
into the grass, forever —
in summer, watching
how a thoughtless landscape
goes on letting itself
be destroyed forever and
ultimately it makes you sad
when you've said Spring
long enough.

GETTING SNOWED IN

Farther and deeper.

Our white steps
fall asleep.

A slow curtain
sinks.

Your pulse beats without a sound
in your wrist.

The cold's at your mouth.

Don't turn around —
I don't want anyone
to find
the snow on our eyes.

THINK I HEARD SOMETHING

Think I heard something. I'm trying
to give it a name.
Some things are worth it.
Shave the rosebeds:
they're too pretty.
Stop your ears.
The Sirens are singing.
"Before we were human
we heard music."
A glass of milk in hand:
describe it. You never
find the right word
for the madness, when you
fold back the wings of
the feminine angels and
squeeze their breasts.
Just do what you will.
People turn their heads
because they don't understand
every death comes differently.
Electronics fails.
You're helpless.
You don't want to live anymore,
and can't.

WINTRY LIFE

I

The reliability of the darkness.

It's a fact that one
hand finds the other more easily now.

Fires are lit
before the eyes of the cold.
The memory of yesterday
is the history of tomorrow:
words freeze in the mouth.
Language dies
at the lips
as smoke.

The crisis of the light persists.
Frost is a singing machine.
Its sound can be heard
through the land.

II

Speak flowers on the windowpane:
it's winter out there.
The sentiments of the landscape
call for patience
with frozen rivers.

True Life
calls itself white.
This child's play with colors,
it's over now.

Notice everything on the way:
between going out and coming back
snow will fall.

BODY

I

Body — meaning
the given, as in
nature — slow automatic
routines, a holding
together, functioning
skeleton, buried
in flesh, that sweats
and loves in the flesh,
changing itself slowly,
grown gray
with even distribution
of heat,
fashioned after
the Golden Mean, working
on another body, wet
and lonely — body
that quickly covers
itself again, bored
by the monotony
of the action but looking
cheerful even at
an advanced age,
joy and happiness aflame

for a long time in it, so
all that's fine and dandy —
an inner drama
trying to get out.
Given its vivid pigment
and the rather homogenous
tissue, its days are
already numbered.
No one ever mentions
its simpleness.

II

For some
it's just an outline for ideas
and as such
a vision of higher things,
physiologically a lie,
disguised as a sound spirit —
body, a sketch
drawn against decay,
carefully arranged
piece by piece,
anatomically perfect,
its organs measurable,
the heart open
and on the X ray
the inner fool,
neither fireproof nor
burglar proof.
Muscles and limbs
live together.
Hand lies down in hand.
The eye sun-like
for poets, all
in all a splendid
sight, while the lazy

conspiracy of time
is at work within, altering
its appearance, ending
its excessive life
at last.

III

Let's see how
it gets along for
a little while,
uninterrupted
by its constitution
or what passes for one.
Accept it as a
complete thing,
let it have its way
with what it wants, waiting
for temporary sensations —
if there's no rush
any time will do. —
Observe its attempts
to escape, the direction
it goes off in
in the sky
or lost in thoughts
about itself
abusing its
qualities:
no mirror of God,
not even a painting
in the mirror, when its
glass reflects it as the imprint

of a special shape,
one motif among others,
mannequin with a soul
that flies from body
to body, dispensing with
health, sticking
to the surface.
It's happy when all
the essential functions
are performed with pleasure.

IV

Utopia, redeemed, freedom
as released tension —
libido that falls back
from object to body
(model of a theory
by sociologists):
when sperm leaves it
in a standing position
or lying down, as usual,
later when it passes water
or on belletristic
walks is overcome
by the landscape,
my friend the year
steps into half-forgotten rooms,
flowers of the season
in arm, while the body
tests finer
faculties, such as potency,
that gleam in its eye
and master of its own house,
from the part in the hair down,
fully formed and taking shape
as if for the first time,
without any impulse or desire for death,

well-being all over
the body, the figure
limber, steady
on its legs without
inclined surfaces.
Natural future has
begun.

V

What's died out
inside it,
used-up sensation,
although the eyes
are restless.
Gradually it takes
on a tangible form
in its weakness:
no longer contradicting
itself.
The fully evolved organs —
good for meditating,
adjusted to the whole.
Chance, like feeling,
done away with. Well-planned
egoism as the art of
loving little,
life as a table
of useless phrases.
Lust still pulls
the body together
sometimes,
before eternity
sets in as a form of leisure.

WINTER POEM

The cold comes from air
that's not hidden by a single leaf.

Fire's disappeared from sight.
Fire's good
for chimneys that send
smoke up.

Each surface grows larger
when it's white.

Whatever can burn
knows about ashes.

Proverbs
are seldom used anymore.

The things we use
are cold and locked in themselves.

We notice when someone
in black clothes walks by.

THE PICTURE WE LEAVE BEHIND

Going off slowly without
anyone noticing.
I don't understand anything anymore.
Opening a door to the night,
not swaying, just leaving
as if nothing could happen.
We leave the picture behind
that some make of us,
with dark spots.
Going off slowly, leaving
our diary behind,
what's been heard, seen, disappears,
we can't correct it,
we lay our will down like
so many names —
night like water
that comes before the falls,
a roaring we
can't make out anymore —
death, that finally took us over
from the life we were leading.

A KIND OF MUSIC

The straight trees, the curved horizon,
the roads quivering in the summer —
an animal that's eviscerated,
the cables like snakes, the wires
in the wind, the bare surface
of the landscape with its eddies of air —
a kind of music if you listen to it,
César Franck, Rédemption,
the wandering lights, evenings,
from your window, behind you
someone waiting in the room
to be able to love you
because nothing happened.